T

space

Japanese Design Solutions for Compact Living

Michael Freeman

UNIVERSE

First published in the United States
of America in 2004
by UNIVERSE PUBLISHING

A Division of Rizzoli
International Publications, Inc.
300 Park Avenue South
New York, New York 10010
www.rizzoliusa.com

2004 2005 2006 2007 2008 /
10 9 8 7 6 5 4 3 2 1

Printed in China

ISBN: 0-7893-1065-1

Library of Congress Catalog
Control Number: 2004102478

Project editor: Noriko Sakai
Consultant: Michiko Rico Nose
Image post-production:
Yukako Shibata

Design by
Claudia Brandenburg,
Language Arts-NY

SEP 2005

introduction

Our endless preoccupation with space—which is to say living space—is an acknowledgment of its role in our well-being. Because dimensions are precise and comparative, space is more often than not assessed in terms of size, and to the Western ideal, at least, larger is better. "Cramped" is a pejorative expression, but significantly it has to do with the experience of the surrounding space rather than its actual physical dimensions. More important is the qualitative use of space, and here it is possible to draw on a different cultural approach. For a number of reasons, both geographical and social, Japan provides some of the most interesting solutions to living in spaces that are more than usually restricted.

Many of these are traditional, although this book concentrates on modern interpretations. In *The Inner Harmony of the Japanese House*, the architectural historian Atsushi Ueda explains one of the basics: "Fundamentally, the traditional Japanese home is a one-room house which has been partitioned into a series of compartments by the *shoji*

(translucent sliding screens made of cedar lattice over which is stretched *washi*, handmade paper) and *fusuma* (opaque sliding screens). This is the major characteristic of space allocation in the traditional Japanese house."

Long before Le Corbusier's famous Modulor, the Japanese were working with a human-proportioned unit that informed not only the dimensions of homes and rooms, but also the way in which they were used. An essential item makes this multifunctionality possible. The tatami mat, a rectangle twice as long as it is wide, is less a mat in the Western sense than a section of flooring, densely woven from blue-green igusa straw, solid enough to be load-bearing while at the same time sufficiently resilient for comfort. Its precise dimensions have changed slightly over the centuries and between regions, but in essence it accommodates one person lying down. There is an old Japanese saying, *tatte hanjo, nete ichijo*, which translates as "half a mat to stand, one mat to sleep." The tatami is no longer ubiquitous in homes, but it survives. It is also, as we'll see in some of the homes here, revived and reinvented in different shapes and styles. During the "bubble" economy years of the seventies and eighties, it fell from favor in the rush to Westernize the Japanese lifestyle as well as economy. In the long, slow recession that followed, many have been rediscovering it.

Of course, the traditional Japanese solutions for living small evolved under circumstances different from those of today—a different social order and a different urban infrastructure. Yet one of the distinguishing features of the best modern Japanese architecture and design is its continuity with tradition. The examples here are naturally not typical of modern Japanese housing, which suffers from the same inadequacies and lack of imagination as elsewhere. It would be useless to pretend that all is harmonious in modern Japan. They do, however, represent the thoughtful and creative approach to living in a compact manner. Most, but not all, are in high-density metropolitan areas—a type of environment that is rapidly becoming interna-tional in its conditions. An underlying theme is the relationship between space and human presence.

In *Empire of Signs*, Roland Barthes wrote, "In the ideal Japanese house, stripped of furniture (or scantily furnished), there is no site which designates the slightest propriety in the strict sense of the word ownership; neither seat nor bed nor table out of which the body might constitute itself as the subject (or master) of a space; the center is rejected (painful frustration for Western man, everywhere 'furnished' with his bed, proprietor of a domestic location)." Throughout, these are Japanese answers, and so perhaps better seen not as solutions to a problem but rather as ways of accommodating the individual to the space he or she inhabits, both physically and perceptually.

enjoy

Attitudes toward size are curiously programmed. Some things are admired for being miniaturized—portable electronic products, for instance. Many more, however, are preferred large—or, to be precise, larger than one has. When it comes to living space, Western ideals tend to be conservatively focused on accretion, which is to say, acquiring more. Indeed, "spacious" is always a term of approval. Material success allows bigger homes, and this expansion of personal, proprietary space is rarely questioned as a good thing.

Yet smallness can be a quality to be enjoyed. The Japanese precedents for this are floor-level living, seated on a tatami mat, and the tea-ceremony room, of which more is discussed later. In restaurants, for example, small rooms— tiny cubicles, really—are extremely popular both for their intimacy and for creating a separate world removed from that of work and the city. And even in working spaces there is a rightness to having just what is needed and within reach. A key component of comfortable, enjoyable small spaces is lightness, whether in the material of construction, the appearance of the structure, or the color. This goes back to the tradition of cedar wood and shoji, and the way in which light is allowed to permeate.

The exemplar of small habitable space in Japanese culture is the *chashitsu*, or tea-ceremony room. The way of tea (*cha-no-yu*) developed as a cult that combined the appreciation of art and simplicity with a striving for purity and harmony or, as Kakuzo Okakura expresses it in *The Book of Tea*, "essentially a worship of the Imperfect." It was refined in the sixteenth century by the greatest of all tea masters, Sen-no-Rikyu (1522-1591), while another tea master, Takeno Jo-o (1502-1555) determined the size of the room as 4 $\frac{1}{2}$ tatami mats. One mat measures approximately 2 feet 11 inches x 5 feet 11 inches, and since the sixteenth century the size of the chashitsu has been compressed to 3 $\frac{3}{4}$, 3, 2 $\frac{3}{4}$, 2, and even 1 $\frac{3}{4}$ mats. This room's space, decoration, and furnishings are central to promoting the ideals of cha-no-yu. "The amount of space was pared to the cramped minimum," writes architect Atsushi Ueda in *The Inner Harmony of the Japanese House*, "because the small space was thought to promote the world of *wabi* (calm simplicity), the central concept in the tea ceremony." Even the entrance is tiny—no more than three feet high. Appropriately named *nijiri-guchi* (wriggling-in entrance), it compels all who enter, whatever their status in life, to bend and be humble.

right: Tea room at the Urasenke Chanoyu Center in Manhattan.

an iconic space

Few Japanese can afford the space that a chashitsu requires in a modern home, small though its dimensions may be. Indeed, few have the time to use one in the traditional way. Nevertheless, the idea of the chashitsu and the cultural heritage that it embodies is regarded affectionately. And as an icon of Japanese sensibilities, particularly with regard to the enjoyment and appreciation of space, it has attracted the creative attentions of architects, designers, and artists. Lacking a strict functionality in the modern world, it has become a vehicle for experiment, a space for reinterpretation with modern materials and design.

above: Tea-ceremony room with a modern curved ceiling, by Shigeru Uchida.
right: Garden leading up to a tea house built on the penthouse roof of a modern Tokyo apartment block.

ambiguity

This modern tea-ceremony room is in a three-story house on a steep hillside near Osaka. The theme here is ambiguity, for the room is not traditional in layout nor is it perfectly clear where the exterior begins. Key to this is the method of division: the corner room is separated inside and outside by a double sliding door instead of a wall. The tatami space

is raised so that it appears to float over the ground, and it is here that the tea ceremony can be performed. The sliding doors, made of Japanese paper and wood, are called *fusuma*, used for partitioning off rooms. When closed, they create the tea-ceremony room, but when opened, the corner space can be used as a Japanese-style veranda, or *engawa*, looking out on a hidden garden of thick-stemmed *mosodake* bamboo. Here is a characteristically vague Japanese space of

left: Tea-ceremony room built into the ground floor of a house designed by Yoshiji Takehara.

half-inside and half-outside, containing views of the room and the garden without clear distinction. The rocky ground in front is the equivalent of an earthen *doma*, which, in a traditional house, is the place for taking off shoes. Here it is a seemingly useless area, which is, nevertheless, a technique for perceptually enlarging space. A second set of glass sliding doors gives a further permutation in the partitioning of this corner section as a closed and open area.

Modern interpretation of a tea-ceremony room with etched glass walls, by designer Shigeru Uchida, in the Mojiko Hotel, Mojiko.

left: The pond garden seen through the open screens.
right: Shadows on the glass walls of the tea-ceremony room.

miniature creation

The corner of a modest-sized garden near Osaka has been converted into a miniature landscape expressly for viewing and enjoying from a light, modern tea-ceremony room. In another example of the rigorous control of viewpoint and the experience of space, the designs of the pond garden and small building have been integrated by the architect Chitoshi Kihara and the garden designer Yasujirou Aoki. The pond, with its carefully chosen rock "island," laps against a beach of gray pebbles, and these, in turn, rise toward the forested mountain of brown granite in one corner. This symbolism, with ferns conveying the wooded slopes and three small trees—maple, camellia, and Japanese oak—representing the forest, is readily understood in Japan. The building is cantilevered so that it "floats" over the pond, and the pillars clad in chromed steel help to expand the space visually. Changing the positions of the sliding translucent screens allows different views over this scene, while the curved wall outside, painted a pale gray to reflect daylight into the area, enhances the sense of infinity. The height of the wall is sufficient to hide the surroundings, even for someone seated on the tatami floor of the room. Overall, there is a gentle but considered use of visual illusion, aimed at assisting the appreciation of miniaturized space.

above and right: The tea-ceremony room and garden, with chromed steel pillar, seen from the lawn in front of the house.

A style of restaurant design now ubiquitous in the popular downtown districts such as Daikanyama, in Tokyo, packs individual rooms into already small spaces. Well-partitioned and connected by narrow gaps navigated by the waiters, nested boxes like this at An Aburiyaki and Sushi Restaurant use lighting and simplicity to avoid claustrophobia. The com- plex includes a bar and two restaurants, but the ultimate destination is intimate. The sense of privacy is combined with the awareness of the sur- rounding action; again, light but effective partition is the key. Japanese use the English word "cozy," but without the fussy, fusty con- notations that it has for a native speaker.

left: Private dining space at An Aburiyuki and Sushi restaurant in Daikanyama, designed by Ichiro Shiomi and Etsuko Yamamoto.

work and play

Imaginative use of materials helps to create enjoyable small spaces in which to work and relax, from the all-aluminum office of architect and designer Toshihiro Suzuki in a fifty-year-old office building to etched steel walls for a tea-ceremony room that serves as a private dining space at fashionable Shunju, a restaurant in Roppongi.

In another restaurant, old branches and white pebbles decorate movable, wheeled rooms. Even when the restrictions of office space preclude even a window, washi paper and natural calligraphy ink, used as a staining for the floor, serve to soften and lighten.

far left: Architect's office with an aluminum theme.
left: Soft, monotone office by Michimasa Kawaguchi.
top right: Individual boxes for dining at Hatago restaurant in Roppongi.
bottom right: A modern steel tea-ceremony room designed by Takashi Sugimoto for Shunju, authentic down to the tiny *nijiri-guchi* doorway.

tatami space

The traditional tatami-mat room—*washitsu* as opposed to the much more specific chashitsu or tea-ceremony room—encourages floor-level living. The tightly woven mats are for sitting and lying on, and induce a lower perspective. In this modern version, architect Ken Yokogawa has inserted twin washitsu into the opened rafters of this new Yokohama dwelling, so that they nestle among the beams like interior tree houses. Instead of a normal ceiling, each has a light, tentlike covering of white lycra stretched upward by a central cord. The guest quarters created are small, light, and airy, yet private.

left: The two adjacent tatami rooms, each with a stretched white lycra ceiling.

Architect Mirai Tono specializes in the use of natural and rustic materials to create the unexpected. Certainly, the downtown office district of Tokyo known as Kanda is not where anyone would expect to find a miniature "earth house" tucked away. From street level, this seven-story office block is typical of the seventies, but inside, on the top floor,

Tono has transformed it into an urban nest—a celebration of nature within the barren, inorganic shell of the building. Mud and straw are the materials of choice for Tono, and he spent three years completing the apartment for himself, his wife, Noriko, and their new baby. The allusions are all intentionally nest-related, and indeed this is the name Tono gave to the home, called Kanda Nest. It follows earlier installations in London and at the Bleddfa Centre in Mid Wales, which also used

mud, straw, and organic forms to give, as he puts it, "spirit to the space." Following the Chinese belief in *chi*, which Tono defines as "the spiritual energy of air," his aim as an artist and architect is to inspire people with its invisible stream.

left: The façade of the office block; the upper floor houses this apartment.
right: Curved mud walls form an inner shell.

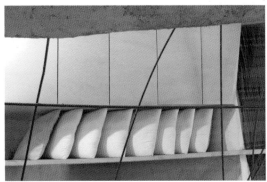

left and top right: The interior as
viewed from the entrance looking
toward the front of the building.
above: Cushion storage between
two mud-plastered panels.

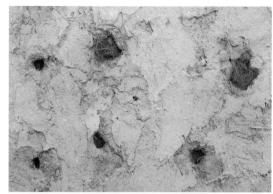

above: Circular openings in the mud walls, some filled with nesting materials as if inhabited by small animals, enhance the organic impression.
right: Truncated and suspended curved beams on the ceiling, one of them lightly plastered.

den. Built in the garden of Kouichi Itoga in three months and at a cost of half a million yen (about $4,600), it features a central hearth for cooking and winter heating, air-conditioning for the summer, tatami mats, a hi-fi system, and a television for watching baseball. It can seat seven people in close comfort. The friends prepared the barrel by leaving it filled with water to remove the smell of the soy sauce. The two-inch-wide boards of Japanese cedar ensure privacy for the Saturday drinking sessions.

With a diameter of approximately six and a half feet, the traditional wooden barrels for the making of Japanese soy sauce are large by any standards, except that of living spaces. In Ibaragi-ken, north of Tokyo and not far from Narita airport, a group of friends who have known each other since childhood conceived the idea of turning one into a weekend

above and below left: Exterior views of the converted barrel in the owner's garden.
above and below right: The *irori*, or traditional hearth, is the focal point of the barrel, used for cooking, preparing tea in an iron kettle suspended from a bamboo pole, and heating sake.

miso barrel
tree-house

Even larger than soy barrels
are those formerly used for
making miso—the ubiqui-
tous fermented soybean
paste—which are featured
in an elaborate construction
near Nagoya. The idea of
John Gathright, who was
born in Oregon and is
active in Japan as an ecolo-
gist and as the founder of
Tree Climbing Japan, an
international organization
for people who enjoy climbing trees, this rambling
tree house is located in a
part of a national forest
in Aichi-ken that is owned
by a Buddhist monastery.
Gathright's concept is "
recycling, zero-emission,
and handmade," using the
huge 140-year-old miso
barrels and old telephone
poles as office space and
home, where he lives with
his wife and two sons.

right: Two of the miso barrels
used as playrooms for the children,
on a raised platform accessed
by ladder.

s
p
a
c
e
36

Miso barrels, which are made from the core of ancient tree trunks, are perfect for the tree house, although the odor was a problem at first. No longer used in miso manufacture, they were never recycled because of the overpowering smell. Gathright spent a couple of years commuting four hours to Nagoya to wash and clean them. Each barrel has a different function. One is the office, where he enjoys reading as well as working. "Inside the barrel is cozy and makes me relaxed. It's the minimum office, isn't it?" he laughs. "It's also a symbol of ecology. I believe we should enjoy recycling." The barrels are round and the main house is pentagon-shaped. "When you decide you are not going to cut down any of the trees, the trees shape your house."

above: The dining room barrel seats five comfortably.
below left: Curved work surfaces in the kitchen barrel.
right: The office barrel is also a connecting space between the veranda and working area.

maximize

There are several ingenious strategies for making the most of small spaces. The starting point—the base strategy, as it were—is to partition the area in such a way as to allow as many activities as possible. The use of different levels is one well-used device; for example, in the form of mezzanines and basements—provided that the access routes themselves take up little space. Ingenuity is key, and this inevitably leads to a pragmatic, ad hoc approach, in which solutions are found on the spot. The miniature step-down elevator in the Akihito Fumita Design office is a perfect example of this.

The partition of space can be temporal as well as spatial, and here the Japanese have a historical advantage in their tatami culture. The tatami is a surface for comfortable living—a resilient area for sitting and stretching out—as much as it is a floor. The consequence of this has been the normality of putting out a futon for sleeping, effecting an instant change of use from living area to bedroom. In the West, the lack of a dedicated bedroom would be seen as a kind of deprivation; in Japan, the tradition is to flip from daytime to nighttime use. Admittedly, this is less common than it used to be, but it retains its popularity with people who are concerned about managing limited space.

right: The bedroom and kitchen occupy the same space in the private half of the apartment.

The couple that lives and works in this tiny apartment in Tokyo's Setagaya chose Makoto Koizumi, the designer of the 9-Tsubo House project (see pp. 66-87), to rework the existing space. Originally, this was a one-room apartment without partition walls, but Koizumi divided the area in such a way that it functions as both home and office. The wooden parti-

tions are less than full height to make full use of the ceiling lighting, and all the partitions function as storage as well, carrying either shelving or cupboards, some of which are enclosed by white plastic. The most distinctive feature of the design is that each subspace has two functions, necessitated by the couple's work. Perhaps the most unusual solution is that the bedroom is paired with the kitchen. A more conventional pairing might have been bedroom with sitting room, but the

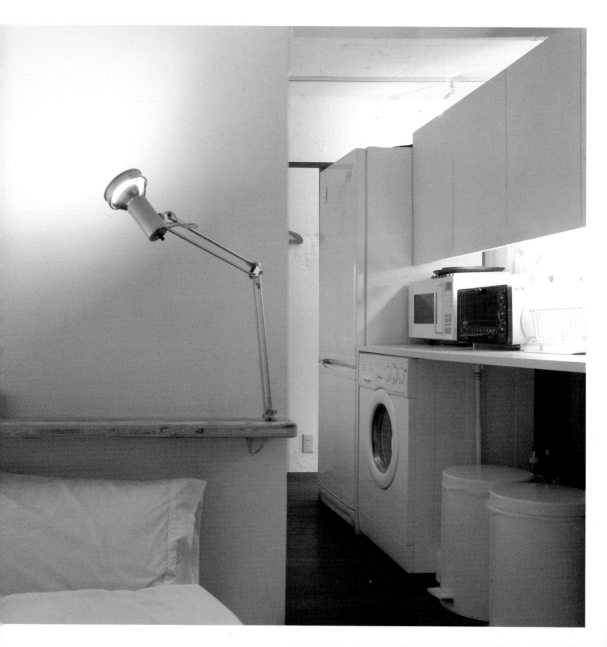

right: The living area with sofa and hi-fi system, viewed from the dining table. Behind the wooden partition is the kitchen and bedroom.

logic here is that food preparation and sleeping are more easily kept separate from the parts of the apartment that receive visitors, whether friends or clients. This arrangement naturally demands extreme tidiness—no dishes are ever left out overnight.

There is a deliberate maze-like quality to the apartment, so that the divisions are partial both vertically (sixteen-and-a-half-foot wooden walls) and horizontally (there is no line of sight between the dining table and the long desk that constitutes the main working area for the couple). Considered touches include the alignment of the natural wood grain of the wall and flooring. This reduces the visual impact of their junction and by softening the edge gives an optical continuity between floor and wall. Other ways in which the division of the space is made to seem less are concealed lighting, such as over the desk, and the interplay of white and natural woods.

left: Immediately inside the
apartment entrance a door opens
into the kitchen; the bedroom
and storage cupboards are beyond.
right: The focal point of the
working area is a long desk with
concealed lighting above.

tiny houses

Although 6 ¹/₂ feet by 19 ¹/₂ feet may seem less than generous for the plot size of a house, these dimensions—322 square feet—are the average that the architect Denso Sugiura works with. Tokyo is full of these small plots, typically reached by lanes hardly wide enough for one car, and the already restricted plan is further squeezed by city zoning laws, which here demand that 30 percent of the area be "exterior." Sugiura has made a specialty of them, and is in demand for his designs of what he calls *chitchai*, or tiny houses. Normally, three floors are possible; the core problem is how to link these in such a way that the tall, narrow home feels like a single space. One of Sugiura's inventive solutions has been to use a tree or tall plant—in one instance a Japanese elm, in another a dogwood, and in another a tall Phyllostachys bamboo—as a linking device.

The common denominator is a small footprint. Sugiura makes sure that the tree plays a part at each level, sometimes as an amenity (as with a surrounding bench for sitting), but always visually. Happily, the tree area, although semi-enclosed, counts as exterior for planning purposes.

left: Expanded steel lathing forms a screen around the decked balcony of the second floor, and a simple square bench surrounds the branches of a dogwood.

The ground-floor area,
also surrounded by expanded
steel lathing, functions
as minimalist garden and
entertainment space.

left: In a second chitchai house in Minato, a tall stand of bamboo provides the vertical link, seen here from the second-floor living room.
right: The open staircase runs up the narrow well containing the bamboo.

s
p
a
c
e
53

The owner of this property, a well-known illustrator, commissioned the architect Manabu Miyama to design a house that would include a suitable space for a studio. In this case, suitable meant not just conveniently placed but also having just the right combination of compactness and spaciousness. The seeming contradiction between these two needs was resolved by creating an attic space in which everything is within easy reach, yet the light and views are open. Miyama made extensive use of glass, and by positioning the studio loft at the rear of the house and slightly separated, it has a kind of aerielike character. The access is very deliberately by means of steep wooden stairs, which clearly divide the living areas of the house and the work space. The owner also likes the sense of "going to the studio to work"; the journey is defi- nite even though short. The studio area could, in fact, have been larger, but as an illustrator he requires a certain degree of privacy to do his work, as well as 360-degree access to everything. Practically, the tiny space is completely convenient, while the airiness eliminates any sense of crowding.

left: Exterior view of the studio loft.
right: Deliberately steep steps help to isolate the studio above from the dining and client meeting area below.

left and above: Everything from art materials to references is within arm's reach, yet the window area is generous enough to give the studio an open feeling.

left: Fitted cupboards and seating for watching television utilize the angle of the sloped ceiling.
right: The reverse view, looking toward the top of the ladder and the living room below.

above left: The family sleep together in a bedroom entirely filled with four futons
above right: the main living area combines dining room and kitchen
below left and right: ladder connecting the kitchen with the boys' playroom above

close family

Architect partners Yoko Kinoshita and Makoto Shin Watanabe, who also designed the house on pages 186 to 187, have a particular interest in designing to meet individual family needs, devising structural solutions that will help to engineer a particular lifestyle. In this property, T.O. House, located in Tachikawa, the objective was to create

both an eclectic mixture of Japanese tradition and Western modern, and family closeness. The owners have two young boys, and at this stage of their upbringing, the parents want to provide a strong nuclear family unit. Undressed concrete with the formwork fittings still exposed was the chosen material; perhaps surprisingly to Western tastes, this treatment, made popular by Tadao Ando and others, remains quite popular in Japan. The boys' playroom has direct access down to

the kitchen and dining room via a ladder. The children have fun using this, and the parents can keep a close eye on their movements. More unusual is the family bedroom, which is one entire sleeping area for everyone. It is good for physical contact between mother and infants, in particular, and also an identical layout to the traditional way of placing futons on tatami mats. In a reversal of normal space allocation, the downstairs entrance is conspicuously large. But by means of floor sections,

these can easily convert from an entrance step to a tatami area; and with a chashitsu "kit" at the ready on the shelf, it has the second function of a modern tea-ceremony room.

left: the surprisingly large entrance area set up for a tea ceremony.
above right: The two floor sections in their typical arrangement, as an area to remove shoes.
below right: Steps leading up the entrance well to the living room. The upper steps lead to the bedroom, bathroom, and playroom.

The office of Akihito Fumita Design was originally a small warehouse for a soap manufacturer and featured a basement. Fumita wanted to make use of this, but with such a limited floor plan, a staircase with returns would have taken up too much space. Also motivated by a desire to make the office interesting and surprising for clients—always an issue in the fashionable design industry—his solution was a small elevator, but without the shaft or indeed anything other than the tiny floor plate and machinery. Placed in the middle of the office, this very undesigned piece of engineering not only opens up the basement for meetings but helps the company convey a practical image.

far left: The basement conference room.
left: The elevator linking the ground floor and basement.
above: The glass-fronted entrance to the Akihito Fumita Design office.

"To design by making an advantage of limited" is an eternal theme in Japan, and the fifty-year history of the 9-Tsubo House project testifies to this. In 1952, the highly respected architect Makoto Masuzawa set out to design "the absolute minimum house," based on a floor plan of 322 square feet. A *tsubo* is a traditional unit of measurement, a square formed by placing two tatami mats side by side. Nine of these form a larger square, but it is still only 18 feet along one side. Masuzawa conceived the idea of a cube with these measurements, and was able to achieve 538 square feet of floor space inside. This even allowed for the *fukinuke*, a vertical space in Japanese construction that connects levels, as in a stairwell or atrium. His principle was that this was "a house that anyone can have built anywhere."

Now this groundbreaking design project has been revived, with the involvement of some of Japan's brightest young architects and designers. Overseen by Yasuyuki Okazaki, who commissions the designs, the project is an experiment in a new and imaginative kind of mail-order housing. The designs are promoted through exhibitions and catalogues; as Okazaki explains, it is the houses that select the customers rather than the other way around. These are individualistic designs revolving around a core theme of minimalism—not the usual way of buying a house in Japan, but appealing to people who share Masuzawa's original ethic of simplicity and necessity.

right: Designer Hisae Igarashi (kneeling) and an assistant assemble a maquette of her entry for the 9-Tsubo House project.

collection house

9-tsubo
house #1

The first of the modern 9-Tsubo houses is located in Mitaka, one of the suburbs of Tokyo. The owner, Shu Hagiwara, deals with interiors and architecture in his publishing business, and when he first came across the project he immediately wanted one. "I just felt like living in this house," he explained, "even though it would be smaller than the apartment I rented at that time." He chose architect Makoto Koizumi to design it according to his own basic idea, and faithfully kept to what he saw as the five basic principles of the original: square plan, 3-tsubo fukinuke, gabled roof with shallow pitch, round pillars, and one principal window at the front.

Avoiding the materials normally associated with inexpensive housing, such as aluminum frames, he chose pine for the flooring and well-finished wood for most of the construction, including built-in furniture. The attention that the house in Mitaka attracted was the encouragement required to take the project further and create a mail-order operation that offered quality and imagination.

left: The exterior of the Mitaka house, the first successor to the fifty-year-old original.

The small tatami room in the
center of the ground floor, used
as a futon sleeping area for
the family. The mezzanine is above.

A simple wooden staircase, open at the side, runs up to the mezzanine. The family uses the mezzanine as a study area.

View from the kitchen across the
ground floor toward the staircase
and side entrance.

9-tsubo
house #2

The second 9-tsubo house to be completed was for a couple in the Shiga district that has a cosmetology and hairdressing business. The building plot that they acquired is large enough for a bigger house, but they fell in love with the minimalist idea, and the all-glass façade gives them a sweeping view across the rice fields to the hills. Long consultations with the architect, Koizumi, resulted in a highly detailed design, again using wood throughout, with built-in storage (see pp. 214-215), a ground-floor tatami room, and upper-floor mezzanine sleeping area. The arrangement of sliding glass windows and shoji screens allows a variety of permutations of light and exposure.

Four variations of the façade. Each of the four windows has a sliding glass panel and sliding shoji screen.

left: View of the two levels
from the head of the stairs, with a
small seating area above and
kitchen below.
right: From the mezzanine looking
toward the bedroom and steps.

left: Tatami room flanked by storage cupboards, behind two wooden pillars.
right: The same two pillars rise through the upper level where they support a rail for the bedroom.

left: With the shoji screens on the ground-floor level pulled back, the dining area extends out to a stone platform that functions as a veranda.
above right: A rectangular slab of black granite is a modern version of the traditional *kutsunugi-ishi*, the stone for removing shoes.
center and below right: At the back of the tatami room, small shoji screens open to reveal another wooden pillar.

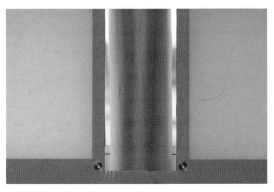

left and right: The doorway at the side of the house, sheltered by a steel awning.

compress

Space restrictions are not only a function of overall size. Shape also matters. Japan, it seems, on the evidence of just walking around the city streets, has more awkwardly shaped building plots than do most countries. Strips and wedges abound, some of them of very unlikely material, and most of them are, for one reason or another, the left-over bits of land from other constructions. This is a condition encouraged by the way in which most Japanese towns and cities have grown, which is to say by accretion rather than following an organized grid system. Odd-shaped urban plots are not uncommon elsewhere in the world, whether due to the encroachment of roads, unusual zoning laws, or family disputes that result in impractical subdivision. The difference is that in Japan there are more people willing to try and make dwelling spaces out of them. Such squeezed spaces are always eye-catching, if only for the "How-on-earth?" reaction that they provoke in passersby seeing them from the outside. Architectural and interior design can go only so far in making use of unusual spaces like these, and they demand a prior commitment by the owners to adjust their lifestyles accordingly.

triangular section

The steep slope of this hill-side plot overlooking the Tokyo suburb of Hachioji is at the limits of practicality for building. The narrow access road that serves several other, conventional dwellings is too steep for vehicles. The architectural partnership of Andrea and Akira Hikone wanted to avoid the usual solutions for leveling because of the limitations that would

result, either raising the front on pillars or cutting back into the slope would lose space and/or light. They chose to experiment with a shape that would actually fit the ground. Instead of fighting the slope, the dwelling makes use of it and achieves stability. There is also an advantage in meeting building regulations, which specify that a proportion of the area remain unbuilt— but only level floor area counts in this respect.

right: The rear of the exterior, looking downhill.

Inside, there are several virtues to the unusual profile—unexpectedly so for the visitor. The strange angle at the back of the house is given over to two rooms. One is a chashitsu, for which the unexpected angles become a feature for contemplation; the other is a double bedroom for the two boys, who enjoy its denlike atmosphere. The several skylights set into the sloping roof make the space bright and airy, while the double-height windows of the façade give maximum enjoyment of the view. The triangular theme is turned into a design motif for the interior, and in the larger sense, the entire house has a strong feeling of spatial orientation, both forward and outward.

left: The boys' room in the rear angle.
above: Adjacent to the boys' room is a small tea-ceremony room.

left: The living area, facing out through the double-height glass façade.
right: The kitchen/dining area.

Central Tokyo is full of
long, narrow, and frequently
useless plots of land
between other buildings.
Known as *unagi-no-
nedoko* (literally, "eel bed"),
many remain abandoned.
This was the case here, in
the heart of fashionable
Azabu, where the architect
couple Tsutomu Matsuno
and Kumi Aizawa acquired
an L-shaped plot of land
that bends behind an

left: Squeezed between two apartment blocks, the building occupies a space not wide enough even for an automobile.
right: The entrance leads into an art gallery.

right: The long entrance is used as a gallery, currently showing an exhibition of photographic portraits.

adjoining building. The previous owner had given up on trying to use the space—it would not even serve as a parking lot. Fortunately, there was plenty of vertical space to play with, and the new owners used this to the maximum, with split levels and a light well located at the angle of the L. They set up a gallery stretching back from the ground-floor entrance to emphasize the workability and openness of the space. The turn at the end of the gallery space surprises with its functional-ity: there is a meeting room and a small garden, the latter of which is at the foot of the light well that rises through three floors. There is an intentional similarity to a tea house and its garden, known as a *roji*. The roji's function is to lead to the tea house. Here, the gallery serves as the roji, the idea of which is to instill a sense of calm and retreat from the hustle and bustle of the city.

Above the long gallery on the ground floor are a partly sublet office on the second floor (which has

right: At the end of the gallery entrance is a small decked garden at the angle of the L-shaped plot, surrounded on two sides by a meeting room and reception area.

two levels) and a bedroom on the third. The office area is startlingly compact, with access to the upper deck by ladder. Aizawa explains, "In fact, the height of the upper office level is only just enough to stand up in. But when we are working, we are normally sitting down at the desk. We spent a lot of time discussing purpose and use before starting to design. If you have a clear idea of the use of a space, a compact design follows logically." Matsuno adds, "Throughout, there are

long-focus views because of the shape, and I've tried to avoid a sense of being oppressed by filling the end with a window." Elsewhere, as much use as possible is made of glass, particularly around the light well. On the ground floor, sliding glass doors allow the small decked garden to become a func-tioning part of the meeting and gallery area in good weather. On the second and third floors, the different rooms and stair-ways wind around the glassed-in well.

left: The light well as seen from the second floor. A walkway leads across to the office area.
right: The third floor is the living area, with the kitchen on the far side and steps to the bedroom leading up on the right. The ceiling doubles as storage for a kayak.

left: The long narrow space facing toward the street, which on the ground floor is occupied by the gallery, is given over to the bedroom on the third floor, with a small terrace beyond.

right: The narrow space below the bedroom is a split-level office, with desk space for several people.

house on a path

Seen from the back, which is the visitor's first view when walking down the lane, this imaginative house near Fujisawa, west of Tokyo, appears incomplete, as if a vertical slice has been taken from another structure. A hillside rises immediately behind it, and one wonders where the rest of the house is. Yet this is exactly the building plot, 131 1/4 feet long but in width tapering from 13 feet to about 8 feet. The grass-roofed structure in the photograph at far left—the bathroom—is almost twice the width of the main dwelling. The story behind this odd site is that it was once a section of the driveway of a large country estate, which has long since disappeared. The owners commissioned architect Takekazu Murayama to come up with a solution. The plot is located at the foot of a steep retaining wall for the adjacent property, and the first step was to negotiate with the neighbors to build right up to this wall. (The Japanese Civil Code demands a 1 1/2-foot gap; under the circumstances this was important enough to bargain for.)

Inside, Murayama avoided partitions as much as possible, to maintain long views through the house and from one level to another. Also, situating the entrance area and stairs in the center made it easier to distribute daylight

far left: The house as it appears from the lane, with the grass-roofed bathroom in the foreground.
left: A Buddleia shrub flowers by the entrance in front of a plastered wall.

left: The view from the workshop across the entrance toward the kitchen and small garden. A toilet fits neatly under the stairs.
right: The reverse view shows the stairs up to the bedroom, with the workshop below.

throughout the house. Perhaps the most distinctive feature is the bathroom, which is made of *hinoki* (Japanese cypress) and is a separate building with a grass roof. A small slender garden leads to it, just as a roji to a tea house, and the experience is that of visiting one of the country-side spa resorts so loved by the Japanese.

The bedroom, with the bed on a raised plinth. On the right, a thick plank catwalk takes the place of steps.

left: The staircase returns outside of the bedroom. After the first step it continues as a sloping plank. **right:** Access to the bathroom, housed in its own building, is across a small garden with stepping-stones.

Yoshiaki Yamashita, an architect with a practice in Osaka, was faced with a challenging site just a short walk from his office. His client's property was on a corner in a typically built-up neighborhood, but due to the way in which the land had been divided between members of the family, the floor plan was not only small and triangular, but reversed, with the project-

ing angle on the inside. This made for an extremely awkward living area, particularly as the owner wanted his shop on the ground floor and three separate apartments for leasing above. Access, fortunately, could be from an exterior staircase. Only one wall was available for windows, and Yamashita used it to the maximum. To further reduce any oppressive feeling from the size (a little under 200 square feet per apartment), he used white combined with the warmth of

unpainted Oriented Strand Board (OSB), which are structural wood panels, for the tiny bathrooms. The kitchen doubles as a dressing area, there is a small drying area for clothes right outside, while the washing machine fits just inside the entrance. Detailing is very important in such a small space; all essentials must fit neatly.

right: The corner property on an intersection of two lanes, with the owner's shop on the ground floor.

above left: The top-floor apartment
with a sloping skylight.
below left: The third-floor apartment,
currently used as a design office.
right: the second-floor apartment,
directly above the shop.

right: The back of the house as
seen from the railroad crossing at
one end of a shopping center.

narrow
as a
virtue

Another "eel bed" building
plot, this time in the north
Tokyo district of Itabashi,
is the survivor of local
municipal planning and
land acquisition. The building does, nevertheless, have
an open view because of
its location near a railroad
crossing and shopping
center. With this in mind, its
architect, Toshiaki Ishida,
decided to make it stand out.
The dimensions are narrow—

52 $1/2$ feet in length but only
5 $1/2$ feet deep—and the site
area is about 452 square
feet. An additional limiting
factor is the planning regula-
tion covering the obstruction
of light on neighboring
properties, which forces the
upper part of the building to
be cut away on a steep
diagonal—a common sight
in urban Japan. Merely an
inconvenience in a large
building, here it completely
dominates the upper floor.

Ishida chose to clad the
entire exterior with stainless
steel, which is in harmony

with the surroundings and
at the same time makes a
strong statement and
changes in appearance with
the light and the viewpoint.
In the same spirit he fitted a
large window in the open
end, where the owner
keeps his bicycle. The interior finish is a textured
cement board painted gray,
to give a soft impression. It
also is highly effective for
both heat and noise insula-
tion. Each floor is designed
as a one-room space, con-
nected by the stair- and
light well near the center.
The most interesting space,

and the one where the owner spends the most time, is the top floor. At one end is the office and kitchen, at the other a relaxation space occupied by a single armchair (there is room for little else). The steep roofline is the defining design element here, and the owner enjoys the distinctive role it plays. In crossing from one end to the other, one is forced to stoop when passing the stairwell, and this is the deliberate equivalent of the nijiri-guchi or "wriggling-in" entrance to a chashitsu (see pp. 10-11).

left: The stainless-steel-clad exterior
at one end of the lane.
right: The window space of the
second floor functions as storage
area for the owner's bicycle.

left: The steeply sloping ceiling
dominates the top floor,
looking toward the sitting area
from the head of the stairs.
right: The same view from further
back, where the office and
kitchen are located.

The reverse view of the top
floor, from the center toward
the office and kitchen.

deep and narrow

The upper floor of this town house, designed as a studio for the artist owner, occupies almost the full width of the property. To ensure that the ground-floor living and dining area would not be dark and gloomy, the architect Yoshihiro Masuko planned a long but, of necessity, narrow garden on one side, to be seen through a wall of glass. The arrangement of lighting in this downstairs area keeps reflections in the glass to a minimum, which helps extend the visual space. The extreme simplicity of the garden—a few shade-loving plants against a large bamboo screen—contributes to the restful quality of the view.

left: A reed screen braced with bamboo dominates the austere narrow garden, seen through the picture window of the living room.

balconies for viewing

Many city apartments are furnished with tiny, impractical balconies, like these two adjoining properties in Tokyo. Too small to offer a seating area, they usually end up underutilized or, worse still, as a place for drying clothes. However, the artist Takeshi Nagasaki decided to seal off the 3 1/4-by-10 foot spaces and turn them into pristine installations to be enjoyed from inside each apartment. Cut bamboo is featured in both, as screens and, in one of the balconies, as a miniature grove. Black bamboo stalks are planted among specially selected white pebbles to give the effect of the edge of a forest in snow. This abuts a pale wood deck. In the other balcony, the flooring is a checkerboard layout of square granite blocks, some of which are sculpted and raised and arranged in a diminishing pattern from right to left. Each balcony is fitted with Nagasaki's trademark lighting of molded glass. In the bamboo-and-white-pebble balcony, some pebbles are in the poured glass, while the lights for the granite garden were molded directly onto the granite surface. The technique involves hand-blowing the glass inside a cubic iron mold so that it takes the form but remains hollow.

above left: White pebbles and black bamboo make a miniature forest scene, with fitted lights.
above right: Glassed-in granite garden viewed from inside the small apartment.
right: Checkerboard pattern of carved granite blocks, with glass lights shaped by the granite surface.

With interior space at such a premium in Tokyo, there is little or none left in modern houses and apartments for those marginal areas used for pleasure and relaxation. One such area is the *engawa*, or veranda, which psychologically enlarges the house. The word has as its root *en*, meaning edge. Takeshi Nagasaki developed some of the themes established in his small balcony gardens here, in a small trapezoidal area of roof in the suburb of Itabashi. Although just large enough to walk into from a door at the top of a narrow staircase—at the top of a slim, tapering building— it is too small for a conventional garden. Nagasaki designed it as part sitting area and part art installation, with built-in objects to be enjoyed for themselves. These include stepping-stones (*tobiishi*) cast in solid glass and in patinated copper. Both bear impressions of bamboo stalks, and the glass tobiishi are lit from beneath at night. In a corner, a ceramic bowl receives drips of water from a green bamboo section built into the wooden bench.

right: A bamboo screen softens the view of surrounding rooftops, while thicker bamboo sections have been used for molding the surface of the copper and glass "stepping-stones."

open

Treating living space as perceptual opens up a number of possibilities, and one of the most interesting is to expand the visual horizons. An apparently straightforward way of achieving this is to do away with conventional partitions, which opens up the available area to its limits. However, just removing dividers is not enough. There is the practical issue of where to put the components that are still needed for living—how to integrate them without their looking awkwardly exposed. There is also the problem of making this single space appear open without seeming empty—a subtle but important distinction. Flexible division, using light and soft materials, is an answer. One special strategy is a legacy of the "borrowed views" of the Japanese and Chinese gardening traditions, in which elements from the landscape beyond are drawn visually into the space by means of careful framing, juxtaposition, correspondence of line and shape, and a measure of control over the viewpoint. The equivalent in modern interior design is to utilize the exterior view through the configuration of windows, glass walls, and sliding screens—and by playing on the ambiguity and uncertainty of the distinction between indoors and outdoors. This is seen at its most radical in the F3 House on page 194-195.

There are two different
kinds of sliding partitions
that have historically played
an essential part in
Japanese interior architecture—fusuma and shoji.
Fusuma are opaque
solid panels, traditionally
painted, while shoji are
lightweight lattice screens
covered with tightly
stretched thin white paper.
The fusuma were room
dividers and cupboard

doors, while shoji were
placed immediately behind
window spaces or along
windowed corridors. What
both have in common is
that they slide in grooves to
open and close. Several of
these in parallel grooves
can partition a large room.
The ease of movement and
lightness of construction
have helped make possible
a culture of opening up
spaces. True doors that
hinge on one side, occupy
space, and are permanent
are alien to Japanese
interior ideas. The fusuma
and shoji are mobile walls,

screens, and windows and in a modern context are constantly being redesigned. In function, they are now used more interchangeably than before.

A variety of sliding partitions, from the traditional (top far left, a fusuma dividing a tatami room in an old *minka*, or farmhouse) to modern. Although the three examples of shoji screens use washi paper, the lattice divisions are non-traditional.

Eels keep cropping up when describing Japanese small-space architecture. They make an obvious metaphor, and the architect Jun Tamaki gave the name to this tall and narrow dwelling near Nagoya. It was yet another example of an unsatisfactory, or at least inconvenient, building plot. The new owners turned to Tamaki because of his ability to develop

imaginative and elegant solutions to this kind of problem. Tamaki was concerned with maintaining privacy when needed but using the verticality of the space to draw natural light down into as much of the two-story house as possible. In a sense, the entire house is oriented toward the sky, while details such as the vertically structured garage doors subtly emphasize this. Indeed, from the street, the most striking aspect of the house is the use of silvered metal shutters on two levels. They

enclose the front half of the building and open dramatically to reveal a view through to the sky from street level (see pp. 142-143) and a view over the city from the living room (see p. 141).

The ground floor has a parking area sufficient for one car and above it is the veranda that extends the living area. The garage roof is an open grille that is also the veranda floor, admitting light to the front bedroom on the ground floor behind the garage. The living area incorporates

desk and computer space for the family, dining table and kitchen, with wide stairs leading down to the children's playroom, bathroom, and bedrooms. The wide stairwell enables light to reach the ground floor, and the steps, lined with bookshelves on one side (see p. 139), are also a space for sitting and reading—they are part of the living area and not just a functional device for moving between floors.

right: Hinged metal screens run on rails around the front projection of the house on both levels.

left: The second-floor living area with the wide staircase on the left.
right: Looking down the staircase to the children's room, with a fitted bookcase along one wall.

left: The front bedroom receives
its light from the open grille of the
second-floor veranda.
right: Looking out across the veranda
from the living area, with the outer
metal screen partly opened.

left and right: The open and closed screens. The steps to the second floor are at the left of the garage space.

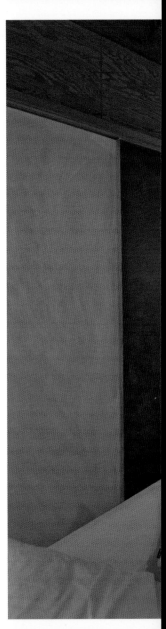

right: One of the two curtains closed on the circular rail, seen from the rear of the house. The front sitting area is concealed.

The Great Hanshin Earthquake, as it is known to the Japanese, devastated Kobe and the surrounding area in 1995 and inevitably resulted in extensive rebuilding. This residential district was damaged less than some other parts, but the family house of the young architect Koichi Sakata needed to be replaced. He and partner Naoto Yamakuma undertook the design and put into practice their own ideas about flexibility of space. Cost was also an important consideration, and this influenced the choice of materials—wood and fabric played the major roles. The bedrooms and bathroom are downstairs at ground level, with the communal living, kitchen, and dining area on the second floor. Sakata and Yamakuma's invention for this continuous space was a circular rail in the middle of the ceiling, from which they hung two light white nylon curtains.

There are several permutations of these, from open to completely enclosed. In the latter case, the table is surrounded and transformed into an intimate dining space, with different lighting moods determined by which lamps are used on the outside. In intermediate positions, the curtains conceal the television and bookshelves from one direction, and the kitchen from another. In addition, sliding wall panels painted by an artist friend cover and uncover a stairway and the recessed kitchen.

left and right: Open and closed, the two curtains can be adjusted to give a different sense of space without appearing to minimize the available area.

The dining area set up as
an enclosed space, completely
surrounded by the curtains. The
kitchen, partly visible, is behind
hand-painted sliding panels.

left: The ground floor, with screened
bathroom and its specially designed
bath with a steam cover.
right: Wooden steps lead up the
narrow space from a small
bedroom on the ground floor to
the main living area.

White polyester curtains are
used in a different way in
this small cubic house
designed by Jun Tamaki. A
series of them on two levels
and of varying lengths
allows many permutations
for the two-story dwelling,
so that the space can be
altered to suit the needs of
a family of four. Tamaki particularly wanted to create a
soft and gentle atmosphere,
and he likens the vertical

folds to the long skirtlike
costume worn by samurai,
the *hakama*, which is the
name he gave to the house.
When all the curtains are
fully closed, the interior
feels, paradoxically, at its
most open and simple.

left: From the upper level, the
view toward the side window
at the top of the steps.
right: A combination of double-
and single-length curtains allows
many variations of open and
closed space.

polygon
and
glass

Karuizawa is a pretty area of forested hills about a three hours' drive north of Tokyo—a popular up-market location for second homes, commonly known as villas in Japan. The owners of this hillside plot wanted something different from the normal spate of Western-style structures being built, and they wanted a space that they could use as a gallery and

left: The entrance porch, approached from a simple rock path.

for entertainment, as well as a weekend house. They had a further request for their young architect, Makoto Yamaguchi: they did not want to use wood visibly. The result was a polygonal capsule of fiber-glass and glass set on a concrete base.

Yamaguchi's answer to flexible use was a single open space, kept visually active by the many angles, in the ceiling as well as the walls, and by the use of glass and mirrored partitions at

right: A picture window gives a
precisely framed view of the early
autumn foliage.

different angles to create
a slightly disorienting
sense of illusionary space.
Multiple reflections
become confused with
transparency. Light enters
through three of the
polygon's surfaces: the
entrance, a window facing
the upslope, and a
huge picture window that
looks out on the famous
Japanese maples of
Karuizawa, which are
spectacular in autumn.
This is a carefully con-
structed view and
was planned from the
start. Because this picture

window projects over
the hillside, the view is con-
centrated on the trees, not
the ground, while the
internal reflecting surfaces
draw the scene and the
light inside. The white and
gray decor helps to emphasize the colors of the hills
and the sculptures dis-
played around the house.

The only room completely
divided from the open area
is the small bedroom.
The bathroom and kitchen
both have glass walls,
and both are partly set into
the concrete base. The

bath is sunken, while
the kitchen has its working
surfaces on the ground,
accessed by an angled
trench with steps down
from the floor at one
end. Although at first
sight there appears to be
little privacy, and there
are no curtains to the
three windows, the siting
of the polygonal house
restricts views from the
exterior. There is a private
pathway on one side,
a precipitous upslope
on another, and uninhab-
ited steep forest on
the picture-window side.

Reflections in the floor-to-ceiling
glass walls interact with the sloping
ceiling sections to create a
geometric pattern.

The bathroom, with its black
sunken bath, is a feature of the
interior design. Glass walls expose
the bathroom to both the interior
and exterior.

left: Steps lead down into the kitchen trench. Storage cupboards for utensils are set into its walls.
right: Kitchen sink, hot plate, and working surfaces are all at ground level.

For his own house in
Setagaya, the designer
Yukio Hashimoto wanted a
combination of privacy and
openness and, as much as
possible in this crowded
Tokyo residential district, a
sense of harmony with
nature. The city skyline, fes-
tooned with overhead
cables, is not particularly
attractive, and the closest
element of nature is the sky.
Accordingly, Hashimoto

designed the house with a
space that is part courtyard,
part terrace extension of
the main living area with a
high exterior wall, so that
the view is of the sky. A
recurring theme throughout
the house is verticality.
He uses various devices to
take the eye upward,
including the tonal arrangement of the "courtyard"
walls, in which the white
upper section blends with
the sky.

An important element in
opening up the living area
is its extension into the

courtyard. Two devices
achieve this. One is the use
of the same wood for the
exterior decking as for the
interior flooring; this and all
the furniture, which was
designed by Hashimoto, is
in chestnut with a natural
finish, and the two surfaces
are on the same level. The
other is full-height sliding
glass partitions that retract
fully behind the wall.

There are other techniques
employed to open the
interior perceptually by
emphasizing verticality. The
doors, some of which slide

right: The simple white façade, and
garage space.

into wall recesses, reach
the ceiling, and this avoids
breaking the line of the
walls. The wooden stair-
case rotates 180 degrees
instead of being in two
straight sections with a
return—again, to maintain
a smooth upward line—
and is enclosed by a glass
wall. In the tea-ceremony
room on the upper floor, the
ceiling is divided into two
levels, each a different
texture, with concealed
lighting recessed into the
gap. This helps to create
a perspective illusion
of greater spaciousness.

left: The living area with floor and furniture in chestnut, all designed specifically for the house.
right: The chestnut flooring is used in the courtyard to expand the space when the sliding glass windows are opened.

left: Ceiling-height doors flanking the entrance hall.
right: A glass wall separates the staircase from the living room.

left: The staircase leading up from the ground floor
right: At the top of the staircase, sliding panels separate the tea-ceremony room from a landing bookcase and bedroom beyond.

above, far left: Table, chair, and slatted kitchen screen doors, all in chestnut.

above left: A niche in the tea-ceremony room, with a small window set into one side.

below, far left: Corner of the courtyard with light fixture.

below left: Modern version of the traditional *mizubachi* (water basin) using a simple tap.

right: The tea-ceremony room with tokonoma alcove and an unusual split-level ceiling.

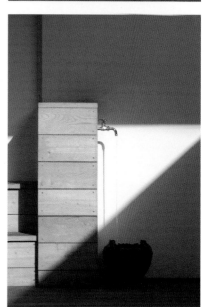

ash house

The specialty of the architect Michimasa Kawaguchi is a reinterpretation of the traditional *sukiya* style to suit modern needs. Sukiya developed with the tea ceremony and is as much a philosophy as a design style, embodying rustic simplicity and austerity. This approach lends itself to opening up small interiors. Two of Kawaguchi's favorite materials are Japanese washi paper and black sumi ink, although he feels free to use them in unconventional ways and to repurpose modern materials and surfaces. For this corner house in Tokyo, named after the single ash tree at its entrance, he discussed the plan and detail with the owner, who is a design consultant. First, they agreed to the minimum use of lines; Kawaguchi believes that "the unconsidered line will make a building look small and stunted." The steps that appear immediately on entering, and which connect the design office on the ground floor to the house above, are plastered in a cream-colored roughened texture using a terrazzo technique. (Terrazzo is a composite material poured in place or precast, which is used for floor treatments.) To this sukiya reference is added a progressive lightening by the insertion of a light well where the steps turn. The use of light to expand the perception of space continues in other parts of the house, notably the bathroom, which has a controlled view of a tiny balcony space constructed as a small garden.

right: The interior staircase leading up from the entrance.

left: The exterior, with an ash tree beside the entrance.
right: The narrow space just inside the entrance is both a lobby for the design studio and a display area with references to a tokonoma.

left and right: The carefully engineered staircase leading from the dining room to the next floor is based on a single steel girder and adds a diagonal, upward component to the space.

left: The bathroom on the top floor uses diffused lighting and simplified fixtures for a soft atmosphere.
right: The view from the bath is of a precisely designed, small balcony garden enclosed by etched glass walls.

Garden design in Japan has long had the status of an art form. One important feature is a recurring two-dimensionality, which comes in the form of framed views, most often a window or other opening from an adjacent building. Framing is one way of controlling the view—it positions the viewer and dictates the spatial relationships. In small houses, where any exterior spaces are also, of necessity, tiny, this is an efficient use of the space available. The gardens in these examples are, on the one hand, too small to enter, but, on the other, sufficient to draw the gaze outward and help, through the illusions of perspective and light, extend the sense of space.

left and right: Three different small garden spaces all treated with the same control over the view, so that each appears as an organized composition.

The slope on which this house was built puts the second floor at ground level at the rear, but also makes the first-floor entrance area a difficult, partly basement-level space. Not surprisingly, it functioned for a number of years as a storage space. When the time came to make something more of it—the owner had decided on a small gallery—the essential prob-lem was light and view. Although eight feet below the level of the garden behind it, the solution from gardener Masayuki Yoshida was to construct what he called a "light-garden," sloping down from the upper-lawn level to draw the light down. The tiny gar-den was constructed on the diagonal, using railway sleepers as steps with which to present seasonally changing plants to the half-underground room.

left: The view from the converted basement gallery.
right: The step garden seen from the normal garden level directly above.

family
living

This house in the Chiba district is a response to the determination of a professional couple to promote a communal family life. Both parents work and the two girls are at school, which erodes the time that the family can be together. Accordingly, the architects Makoto Shin Watanabe and Yoko Kinoshita, who also designed the house on pages 60–63, created a spatial organization that severely restricts the private areas. The communal areas—kitchen, dining area, study, and living room—are spacious, in contrast to the private rooms, which have space for little more than a bed. Kinoshita's term is "micro-bedroom," and the idea is to counter the modern trend for fully equipped children's bedrooms that are partly responsible for a growing "isolation syndrome" in Japanese society. The laundry area is also communal; everyone has responsibility for his or her own clothing. After washing, clothes go onto mobile racks for drying, where they are ready for wearing. There is no enclosed storage space.

left: The communal laundry and clothes storage area.
right: Individual walkways lead to each of the small bedrooms.

s
p
a
c
e

open
plan

Removing internal walls is
an established technique
for dealing with space, but
in the case of the architect
Kiyoshi Kasai's home, the
concept has been extended
by dispensing with all internal structural supports, and
by raising the ceiling to
about 16 ¹/₂ feet, which,
given the low ceilings that
most Japanese are accus-
tomed to, is even more
expansive than it would be

in the West. For the family,
whose individual bedrooms
are small, functional, and in
an adjoining small building,
this is an all-purpose area
with fluid functionality. The
curved central wall contains
the kitchen below and a
study/play area above,
while the use of canvas and
wood further increases the
sense of openness.

left: Wooden bracing on the ceiling
and walls allows the space to be
free of pillars and structural walls.
The curved unit on the right houses
the kitchen below and a concealed
study above.

s
p
a
c
e

189

surprise
value

By most standards this tiny apartment is an intractable space for design. Measuring just 312 square feet, with no view to speak of other than the freeway a few feet away, it is all too typical of apartment housing in Japan. And before this owner moved in it had actually been divided into three rooms. The interior designer Toshihiro Suzuki elected to overcome the

apartment's shortcomings and claustrophobic appearance by stripping everything down to the structure, including wall plaster. The surfaces are naked, and the furnishings are constructed almost exclusively from water pipes. The renovations were inexpensive, are highly functional, and sufficiently innovative to distract attention from the small dimensions.

left: All the fixtures, including shelving, are constructed from water pipes; taps are used as stoppers.
right: The bathroom is shielded by a screen of vertical pipes clad with translucent corrugated plastic.

s
p
a
c
e
190

far left: The complex shape of the glass and steel bathroom (there are no right angles) dominates the interior space.

left: Suspended in one upper corner of the two-story space is the daughter's bedroom, also in glass and steel.

inverted privacy

The bulk of the area of this new house in Funabashi, just northeast of Tokyo, is a multifunctional two-story space. Nothing radical about that, except that the architect Norisada Maeda, who has something of a mission against the conservatism of most Japanese housing design, decided to make the bathroom its central, transparent focus.

On one side is the living area, on the other the kitchen and dining table, and above is suspended the daughter's bedroom, reached by a staircase and catwalk. All of them look into this 10-foot-tall plate-glass structure, which has no right angles. For the visitor, it has a disconcerting lack of privacy. But the family is close, and the owner in particular likes to sit in the bath and watch life going on around him.

space

193

open to
everything

Taking openness to an
extreme, the architect
Koh Kitayama fulfilled this
client's request for a
house in which the living
area and utilities would
be at a minimum, so
as to devote the remainder
to "entertainment"
space. His radical solution
was in the form of two
intersecting geometrical
shapes: a long, square-
sectioned box inserted

s
p
a
c
e

left: The living module, though tiny, opens out onto a large, airy space.
below left: The upper floor functions as a glassed-in terrace.
right: The three-story structure is almost totally exposed, with the exception of the living module, part of which projects out at left.

into a gabled structure. The surprise is in the materials chosen. The living "box" is all privacy when wanted, being fronted with sliding screens, while the main house is a giant glass structure— front, top, and sides. There is a sense of being able to afford to squander space, which perceptually adds to the volume. Sliding back the screens opens up the space remarkably—into the street and, in fine weather, as far as Mount Fuji on the horizon.

conceal

The accumulation of possessions is an international constant and brings with it the issue of where to keep them. This is all the more urgent if space is limited. In comparing the Western and Japanese storage traditions, the former has been likened to a "museum" culture and the latter to a "theater" culture, reflecting two quite different attitudes toward the movable items of a home. In the museum approach, there is a series of units and surfaces filled and stacked with implements and objects. The degree to which they are loaded varies according to taste and fashion, from say Victorian bric-a-brac to Scandinavian pine and steel, but there is an underlying similarity: a visible set of cupboards, shelves, and cabinets are a functioning part of the interior. In the theater culture, by contrast, a few objects at a time are brought out as required, either for display as in the tokonoma alcove that reflects the changing seasons, or for mundane tasks such as the utensils needed for food preparation. They are then returned to a hidden area of storage, out of sight. The corollary of the theater approach, therefore, is concealment—the backstage of the living space.

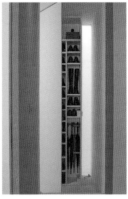

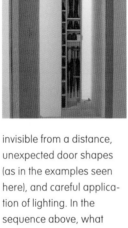

Even in a Japanese house it is hardly possible to dispense with cupboards. The design problem is how to remove them from attention when they are closed and yet present them in a visually acceptable way when they are open. The art of hiding them from view lies in the detailing and draws on a number of techniques, including precision in the fitting to make joints invisible from a distance, unexpected door shapes (as in the examples seen here), and careful application of lighting. In the sequence above, what appears to be a wall is, in fact, a shoe cupboard, and this concealment is achieved with a door that is slightly wider on the right edge than the cupboard. The lighting arrangement of a small window behind and a single-spot downlighter on the cupboard door add to the illusion that this is a wall rather than a cupboard.

above: Shoe cupboard in the Ash House.
below: The diamond-shaped spaces between wooden wall braces in the house on pages 188–189 are cupboards, accessed by hinged triangular doors.
right: A cubic display niche is surrounded by storage space for other objects.

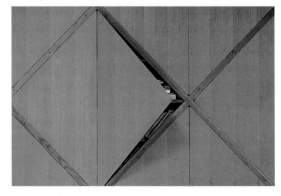

A simple but highly effective way of appropriating more space in an interior is to suspend objects and storage units. To avoid a visual sense of crowding, this needs to be done with care. A good example of this is the hanging cupboard in a kitchen designed by Shigeharu Isaka. Open kitchens with freestanding units have become popular in Japan in recent years,

and in this case the unit, in translucent polycarbonate, is suspended directly over the sink. The other two examples make use of concrete walls. In a house in Sapporo, also by Isaka, the slippers that are always provided to visitors at the entrance to a Japanese house are offered in a basket, rather than being left on the floor as is typical. The recessed circular formwork fixtures in undressed concrete make a convenient location for hooks, used here in a house in Sapporo designed by Yoshio Maruyama.

When a Kyoto couple
commissioned the architect
Jun Tamaki to design a
smaller house to which they
would retire, it was determined that there would
not be sufficient space for
their large library. Rather
than reduce the collection,
Tamaki decided to put
it all into storage save for
one favorite book—on
Matisse—that would stand
in memory for all of them.

Tamaki created a fitted
niche in the thick wall. In
Hashimoto House (see
pages 164-173), books are
dealt with in a different
way. The same naturally-
finished chestnut that helps
give continuity to the living
room and terrace runs
through the house, and the
staircase has fitted drawers
set into the risers.

left: Wall niche for a single volume.
right: Drawers fitted into the bottom
three risers of the staircase.

bookcase, while in the Eel House (see pages 136-143), the shelving neatly conforms to the staircase.

Books and steps have a habit of going together. The traditional *Kaidan tansu*, a step-chest that functioned as staircase as well as storage, has been made over in plywood (opposite) in Kazuhiko Namba's design, with open cupboards and a repetition of squares. In the house that appears on pages 106–113, the wide lower step leading up to the bed opens to reveal a low

left: Modern plywood version of a step-chest makes maximum use of the space available.
above: Book and magazine storage set into the broad step leading up to the bed in the house on pages 106 to 113.
below: Bookcase lining the broad steps in the Eel House.

sliding
staircase

This simple idea is beauti-
fully executed, both in the
way it works mechanically
and aesthetically. A retract-
ing ladder staircase is
a solution to maximizing
the storage space in a
house on the northern
island of Hokkaido. It gives
access to the attic at the
same time as fitting neatly
into the concealed wall
storage units. Unlike most
ladders that swing up or

down or fold, the architect
Yoshio Maruyama
designed this metal one to
slide sideways on tracks.
When folded away it is
flush with the wall, where
the cupboards have been
designed in triangular
sections to accommodate
it. Painting the staircase
red makes it a strong design
feature of the square
side wall.

above: The steel ladder slides out on
a ceiling rail.
right: When closed it becomes
a design feature of the wall, dividing
the triangular cupboards.

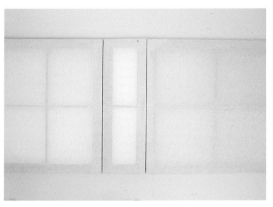

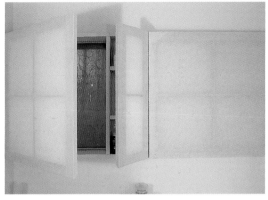

Sliding screens and doors have uses other than partitioning rooms. In the apartment of a retired couple living in Ofuna, a tiny but convenient study is built into a wall recess in the bedroom, revealed by sliding doors. Alternative applications for washi paper, normally used for shoji screens, have been found by the young architect Arata Naya, who uses the same construction of paper stretched tight over a light wooden frame, but for Western-style doors and windows.

left: Study revealed by sliding panels in an Ofuna apartment.
right, above: Shoji-constructed hinged screens for a window.
right, below: Shoji construction used for a Western-style door.

On the second floor of this
house in Sapporo designed
by architect Yoshio
Maruyama, the aim was
to maintain a sense of
openness. One result was
that the access from bed-
room to bathroom crosses
an area potentially visible
to other people. Maruyama
installed three fabric roller
blinds so that they can, as
much as is needed, be
lowered to afford privacy.

When all three are com-
pletely lowered, they make
a pale, translucent box.

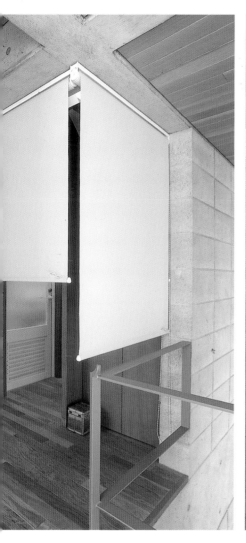

toilets

In the Villa Karuizawa (see pages 154-163), the toilet is concealed in a clever use of reflection. Located at one end of the bathroom, it is separated by a two-way mirror. This transmits only about a tenth of the light in one direction, so that in daylight all that is visible from the bath and the rest of the open area is a mirror wall-one of many reflecting surfaces in this interior. In

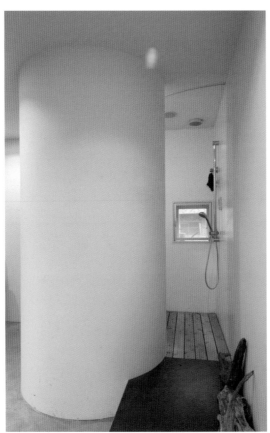

the narrow angled gallery/office/home on pages 96 to 105, the solution has been to hide the toilet in a return behind a circular wall that appears to be a pillar. The bath itself is treated here as a focus of

attention, built into the concrete base.

above: Toilet concealed behind a false pillar.
right and far right: In the Villa Karuizawa, the toilet is concealed by a two-way mirror in an otherwise transparent house.

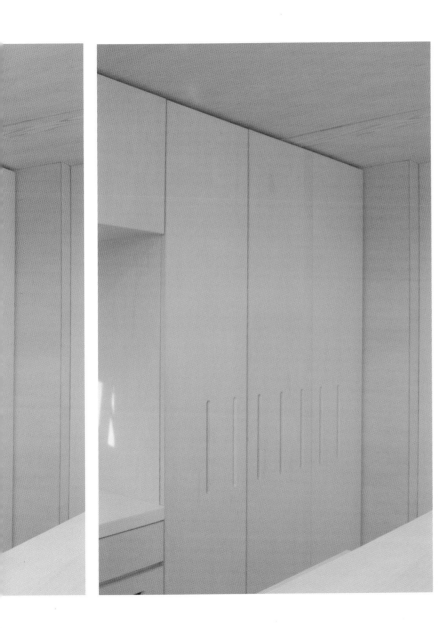

Sliding
Shelves

In the 9-Tsubo house in
Shiga (pages 76-87), the
kitchen shelves are arranged
perpendicular to the wall,
into which they slide, flush
with other, more convention-
ally arranged cupboards.
While there is no saving on
physical space, the two
advantages in this tiny house
are perceptual (through
concealment) and access,
as they require no perma-
nent space in front of them.

Another space for concealment in the Villa Karuizawa is the concrete base, which, on the side facing down the hill, allows recessed storage. Rather than hide the hatch leading down to this cellar space, the architect used toughened glass in a metal frame to match the extensive use of glass partitions and windows elsewhere. Even more original is the

kitchen trench, entered from one end down a short flight of steps. Utensils are stored in cupboards set into the walls of this trench, but with everything painted black there is no view from above.

above: Floor-level kitchen behind a glass wall.
right: Floor hatch in toughened glass gives access to cellar storage space.

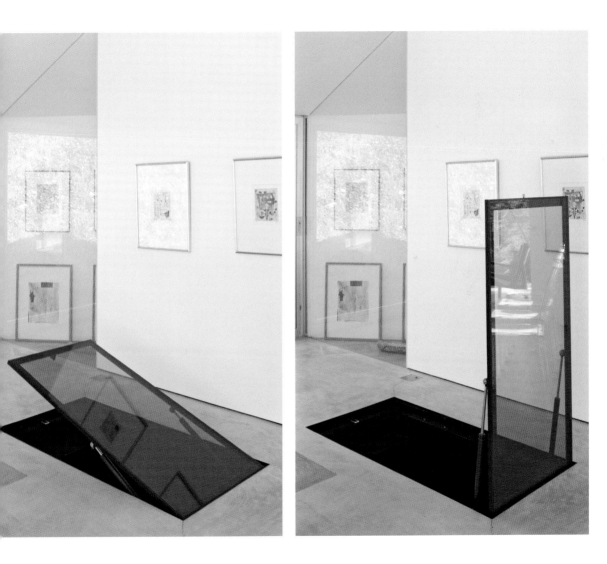

hatches

More uses for floor hatches in facilitating the movement of furniture. In the Kobe house on pages 144–151, the hatch opens to a straight drop to the ground floor, enabling furniture to be hauled up. In the steel-clad house on pages 118–125, the hatch simply extends the area above the staircase.

left: Floor hatches in the house featured on pages 118 to 125.
right: Hatches to the entrance area in the wooden floor of the house on pages 144 to 151.

futon
store

The traditional use of futons for sleeping, spread out on the tatami floor at night and packed up each morning, makes a bulk storage space essential. This is known as *oshiire*, and is normally a cupboard with a sliding door. In one of his Chitchai houses (two others are featured on pages 48–53), Denso Sugiura devised this ingenious alternative; at the touch of a wall switch, an electrically operated jack raises one tatami mat to reveal the futon. In the 9-Tsubo House in Mitaka, the even smaller tatami room on the ground floor was given small square tatami mats by Makoto Koizumi, in keeping with the square modular design. These hinge upward for access to storage space beneath.

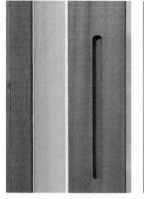

detail
and
finish

One notable feature of Japanese design in all areas is the attention to detail. This has as its roots in the understanding that design elements are seen and used at more than one scale. A door or screen or cupboard has its place within the overall structure of a room, but in its function—opening and closing—it also has a presence at a distance of

just a few inches. The projection of a doorknob, the recessed grip in a sliding door, a light switch, and even a basic electrical socket can detract from the visual harmony of a living space if they are poorly executed or too prominent. Thoughtfully designed fittings at a detailed level are evidence of care in the design at a larger scale, and provide a high degree of satisfaction— all the more so in small spaces where they are especially evident.

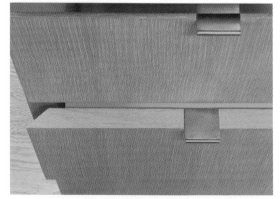

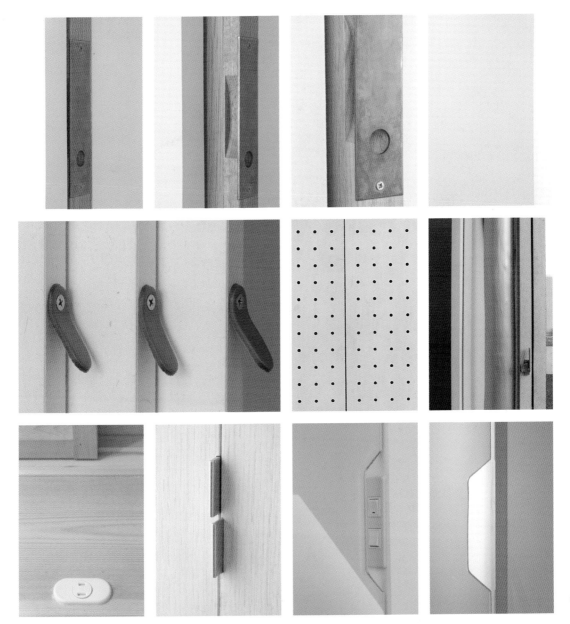

acknowledgments

Kumi Aizawa
An Aburiyaki and Sushi
Restaurant
Yasujirou Aoki
John and Hiroko Gathright
Akihito Fumita
Shu Hagiwara
Yukio Hashimoto
Andrea and Akira Hikone
Hisae Igarashi
Shigeharu Isaka
Toshiaki Ishida
Kiyoshi Kasai
Michimasa Kawaguchi
Chitoshi Kihara
Yoko Kinoshita
Koh Kitayama
Makoto Koizumi
Norisada Maeda

Yoshio Maruyama
Yoshihiro Masuko
Tsutomu Matsuno
Manabu Miyama
Mojiko Hotel
Takekazu Murayama
Takeshi Nagasaki
Kazuhiko Namba
Arata Naya
Yasuyuki Okazaki
Gyoko Osumi
Akira Sakamoto
Koichi Sakata
Ichiro Shiomi
Shunju Restaurant
Takashi Sugimoto
Denso Sugiura
Toshihiro Suzuki
Yoshiji Takehara

Jun Tamaki
Mirai Tono
Shigeru Uchida
Makoto Shin Watanabe
Makoto Yamaguchi
Naoto Yamakuma
Etsuko Yamamoto
Yoshiaki Yamashita
Ken Yokogawa
Masayuki Yoshida